Just Like Me

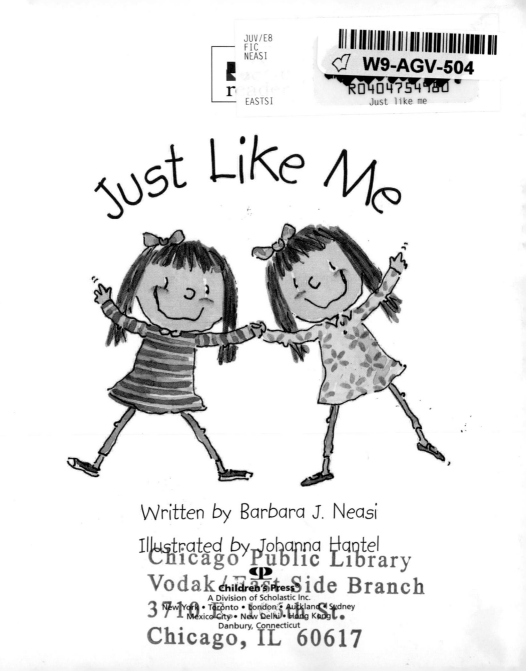

Written by Barbara J. Neasi

Illustrated by Johanna Hantel

Children's Press
A Division of Scholastic Inc.
New York • Toronto • London • Auckland • Sydney
Mexico City • New Delhi • Hong Kong
Danbury, Connecticut

For Jennifer and Julie—my identical inspirations
—B.J.N.

To my parents
—J.H.

Reading Consultants

Linda Cornwell
Literacy Specialist

Katharine A. Kane
Education Consultant
(Retired, San Diego County Office of Education and
San Diego State University)

Library of Congress Cataloging-in-Publication Data

Neasi, Barbara J.
  Just like me / written by Barbara J. Neasi ; illustrated by Johanna Hantel.
      p. cm. — (Rookie reader)
Summary: Jennifer tells of the many ways that she and her twin sister, Julie, are alike and
different.
  ISBN 0-516-22669-X (lib. bdg.)   0-516-27495-3 (pbk.)
  [1. Twins—Fiction. 2. Sisters—Fiction. 3. Individuality—Fiction.] I. Hantel, Johanna, ill. II. Title.
III. Series.
  PZ7.N295 Ju 2002
  [E]—dc21

                                                                          2001008321

CHILDREN'S PRESS, AND A ROOKIE READER®, and associated logos are trademarks and or
registered trademarks of Grolier Publishing Co., Inc. SCHOLASTIC and
associated logos are trademarks and or registered trademarks of Scholastic Inc.
    4 5 6 7 8 9 10 R 11 10 09 08 07 06 05 04

My name is Jennifer.
I have a twin sister.
Her name is Julie.

3

She has long brown hair.
Just like me!

She has big brown eyes.
Just like me!

Julie is in first grade.
Just like me!

She goes to dance class.

Just like me!

She likes to roller-skate.
Just like me!

She likes bubble gum.

Just like me!

She sleeps in a big bed.
Just like me!

Julie has a kitten.
Not like me!

She likes to clean house.
Not like me!

Julie likes to float on the water.
Not like me!

She likes to wear dresses.

Not like me!

She likes pancakes.

Not like me!

Julie likes to wear black shoes.

Not like me!

Julie wakes up early.
Not like me!

Sometimes we are the same.
Sometimes we are different.

But we are always twin sisters!

Word List (58 words)

a	different	her	me	sleeps
always	dresses	house	my	sometimes
are	early	I	name	the
bed	eyes	in	not	to
big	first	is	on	twin
black	float	Jennifer	pancakes	up
brown	goes	Julie	roller-skate	wakes
bubble	grade	just	same	water
but	gum	kitten	she	we
class	hair	like	shoes	wear
clean	has	likes	sister	
dance	have	long	sisters	

About the Author

Barbara J. Neasi is a children's writer, a substitute teacher, and a mother of four daughters. Two of them are the twins, Jennifer and Julie, who are alike and different at the same time. Now that the girls are all grown up, Barbara lives in Moline, Illinois, with her husband, Randy, Tyson the dog, and Peanut the cat in a little gray house with a big garden, where her grandchildren pick flowers and pumpkins.

About the Illustrator

Johanna Hantel has been creating silly, squiggly drawings since she was very little. Her parents' house is her gallery. Her cat, Franklin, models for her. In her spare time, she likes to run very long distances.